THIS BOOK BELONGS TO:

_____

Copyright © 2021 Nakia M. Evans

ALL RIGHTS RESERVED.
No part of this publication may be reproduced, distributed, or transmitted in any form or by any means, including photocopying, recording, or other electronic or mechanical methods, without the prior written permission of the publisher, except in the case of brief quotations embodied in critical reviews and certain other noncommercial uses permitted by copyright law.

Disclaimer: The information contained herein is general in nature and for informative purposes only. It is based on the author's personal experience. The author assumes no responsibility whatsoever, under any circumstances, for any actions taken as a result of the information contained herein.

THE PRINCIPLES of LEADERSHIP

NAKIA M. EVANS

Note from the author

I am dedicating this book to my children.
I want them to always remember that I became a Leader to provide them with the life of their dreams.

You are the prize.
You are MY prize.
Dream BIG!
Think BIG!
Go BIG!

Believe in yourself more!
There are no shortcuts to success. Always be willing to do something that will change your life. It's Beyond where you are now.

Always refuse to believe that you are bound to anything that puts a limitation on what you can achieve.

Honor & Love yourself first!
I Love You!

TABLE OF CONTENTS

WHAT IS A LEADER?

CHAPTER #1: THE SELF-MOTIVATED LEADER

CHAPTER #2: THE CONFIDENT LEADER

CHAPTER #3: THE ACCOUNTABLE LEADER

CHAPTER #4: THE PASSIONATE LEADER

CHAPTER #5: THE COURAGEOUS LEADER

CHAPTER #6: THE LEADER WITH INTEGRITY

CHAPTER #7: THE EMOTIONALLY INTELLIGENT LEADER

CHAPTER #8: THE HUMBLE LEADER

CHAPTER #9: THE VISIONARY LEADER

CHAPTER #10: THE DISCIPLINED LEADER

CHAPTER #11: THE COMMUNICATING LEADER

KNOW, GO & SHOW THE WAY

BONUS: 8 DAILY HABITS OF OUTSTANDING LEADERS

Before we get into the nitty-gritty of effective leadership, let's make sure we're all on the same page regarding what a leader actually is. There are a thousand definitions of leadership, and we want to ensure that we're all speaking the same language. Generally speaking, a leader is someone who motivates others to act toward achieving a common goal. A leader is able to rally people around a cause and move them to take action toward achieving a particular objective.

A good leader inspires people to do something bigger than themselves. To work together to accomplish key objectives. To pool their strengths and resources to achieve great things. A good leader helps their team members become the absolute best version of themselves. Winston Churchill, in inspiring the people of England to keep fighting in WWII, is a great example of leadership. Thanks to his inspirational leadership, the people of England made great sacrifices in their fight against the evil Nazi regime.

A leader is different than an organizer. An organizer gathers resources and deploys them in the most effective manner. Yes, an organizer brings people together, but they don't inspire them to take big, bold action.

Organizers are about efficiency while leaders are about vision.

What traits and talents characterize a good leader?

HERE ARE 7 HIGH-LEVEL CHARACTERISTICS:

VISION

An effective leader has a clear vision of where they want to go and how they're going to get there. They understand where they currently are and are crystal clear on what it's going to take for them to get to where they want to be. The leader must be able to communicate this vision clearly to his team.

MOTIVATION

The effective leader is highly skilled at motivating people. They know what makes others tick and are able to tap into those emotional triggers. Through their words and actions, they are able to motivate people to do things they maybe wouldn't do otherwise

SERVICE

The best leaders are those who serve their followers. They seek to serve their team and make their team as effective as possible. They support their team members in whatever ways they can rather than constantly focusing on their own agenda and what they want to accomplish.

EMPATHY

A leader must be able to place themselves in the shoes of others. If they want to create consensus among their team, they must be able to understand the concerns of others and effectively respond to those concerns.

CREATIVITY

The highly effective leader is creative when it comes to achieving their outcomes. They use their imagination to look beyond what is directly in front of them to see what's truly possible. They're able to see how they can effectively leverage the skills of their followers for the maximum good.

DEMANDING

The best leaders demand the best from their teams. They don't settle for mediocre results or half-hearted efforts. Rather, they set an example of passionate work for their team, and they expect their team to follow their example.

MANAGEMENT

A leader must be able to manage those who follow him. They must be able to strategically guide their team through complex processes, effectively resolve challenges they encounter, and marshal the resources of their team to be deployed for the most good.

None of these characteristics on their own makes for a good leader. The best leaders possess a combination of some, if not all of these characteristics.

They are able to be both creative and demanding at the same time. They can manage effectively while also expressing empathy for their team members. They can provide vision while serving their followers at the same time

It's important to understand that leadership isn't about having a particular position, title, or personal attributes. Just because you're an executive doesn't mean you're a leader. Having the corner office doesn't mean you're good at leadership. Having a charismatic personality doesn't make you a leader.

Kevin Kruse puts it this way:

> **LEADERSHIP IS A PROCESS OF SOCIAL INFLUENCE, WHICH MAXIMIZES THE EFFORTS OF OTHERS, TOWARDS THE ACHIEVEMENT OF A GOAL.**

The good news is that leadership is NOT something you're born with. Rather, it's something you learn over time through practice. And you can become a better leader than you currently are.

If you're not an effective leader now, you can grow and become an effective leader. You can learn the skills and techniques necessary to have the social influence Kevin Kruse talks about.

That's what this eBook is all about. In this book, you'll discover 11 principles of highly effective leadership.

Ready to dive in?

Let's get moving!

WHAT IS A LEADER?

What is a leader?

What is the difference between a leader and an organizer?

Why is being a leader NOT about having a specific title or position?

What are some of the characteristics of an effective leader?

Is leadership a skill you're born with?

First and foremost, a leader is self-motivated. Unlike followers, who must be told what to do, a leader is someone who is highly self-driven and motivated.

A leader is out in front of the crowd. They are moving forward on their own initiative, taking action without being told to do so. A leader must be able to drive things forward without the approval or permission of others.

They must have an innate desire to make change happen, even when they can't see exactly how it's going to happen.

A leader isn't primarily motivated by salary or social perks. They have a fire within them. A powerful desire to make good change happen.

Daniel Goleman puts it this way:

PLENTY OF PEOPLE ARE MOTIVATED BY EXTERNAL FACTORS, SUCH AS A BIG SALARY OR THE STATUS THAT COMES FROM HAVING AN IMPRESSIVE TITLE OR BEING PART OF A PRESTIGIOUS COMPANY. BY CONTRAST, THOSE WITH LEADERSHIP POTENTIAL ARE MOTIVATED BY A DEEPLY EMBEDDED DESIRE TO ACHIEVE FOR THE SAKE OF ACHIEVEMENT.

HOW CAN YOU GROW IN SELF-MOTIVATION?

The primary way is by choosing a goal (or set of goals) that resonates with you deeply and stirs you up to want to accomplish great things.

Think about your own life and career. What sorts of things do you really, truly want to accomplish? **What goals set you on fire** and make you want to take massive action? What objectives would you be willing to sacrifice for?

It's these kinds of things that create motivation. Focus your attention on them. Write them down. Rehearse them again and again. **The more you're focused on your big, audacious goals, the more you'll be motivated to want to achieve them.**

Assuming your goals involve more than just yourself, you'll also be motivated to get others on board with your goals.

THE SELF-MOTIVATED LEADER

What does it mean that a leader is self-motivated?

How can you grow in self-motivation?

What are the goals and objectives that drive your motivation?

Do you feel like you're lacking in motivation? What steps can you take to change that?

If you want others to follow you, it's absolutely essential that you be confident, both in your overall vision and the approach you take to making that vision a reality.

What exactly is confidence? It's an inner belief that you have the ability to achieve what you set out to do. It's the personal assurance that you can accomplish whatever you put your mind to. It's the feeling that nothing is too big or challenging for you.

But isn't confidence something you're born with?

Not necessarily.

Confidence is born out of action.

In other words, the more action you take, the more overall success you'll have. The more success you have, the more confident you'll feel, which will lead you to take more action. This leads to more confidence, and this positive cycle continues.

Yes, there will be times that you fail. There will be times when your ideas don't pan out and your best efforts fall flat. There will be times when even your best-laid plans go to pieces.

In those moments, you'll be tempted to give up. Your confidence will flag, and you may doubt your ability to accomplish things.

Avoid giving in to that temptation! If you want to be a confident leader, **it's absolutely critical that you keep taking action, moving forward, and striving for your goals.**

Winston Churchill said, *"Success is not final, failure is not fatal: it is the courage to continue that counts."*

It's the courage to continue taking action that makes for a great, self-confident leader. The best leaders are inherently confident, and they're confident because they've consistently taken action.

THE CONFIDENT LEADER

What does it mean to be a confident leader?

How is confidence born out of action?

Why is it so necessary to keep going even when you fail?

If you want to be a highly effective leader, you must hold yourself accountable for both your actions and the outcomes that those actions produce.

When things go well, you take appropriate credit (and give credit to your team, of course). When things don't go well, you take the blame. You're the leader of the team and, therefore, everything ultimately falls on you.

The opposite of the accountable leader is the "victim" leader. The victim leader blames everyone and everything else for their failures. They refuse to believe that their actions could result in any problems and so they constantly blame their challenges on others. They may take credit for successes, but they don't accept the blame for failure.

If you're going to be a powerful, compelling leader, you must accept 100% responsibility for the outcomes of your actions. You must take decisive action to influence specific outcomes and then embrace those outcomes, whatever they may be.

Deep Patel puts it this way:

> **EFFECTIVE LEADERS HOLD THEMSELVES ACCOUNTABLE AND TAKE RESPONSIBILITY FOR THEIR OWN MISTAKES—AND THEY EXPECT OTHERS TO DO THE SAME. THEY CAN WORK WITHIN ESTABLISHED PROCEDURES, AND BE PRODUCTIVE AND EFFICIENT IN THEIR DECISIONS.**

If you don't hold yourself accountable as a leader, how can you expect to hold others accountable? If you aren't willing to set a high bar for yourself, how can you set a high bar for those on your team?

The reality is that your followers will never rise higher than you. They will look to you and follow your example. If they see you constantly blaming others and refusing to be accountable, they'll do the same thing.

Work hard to hold yourself accountable and your team will do the same.

THE ACCOUNTABLE LEADER

What does it mean that a leader must be accountable?

Why do the most effective leaders hold themselves accountable?

What is a "victim" leader?

Do you accept 100% responsibility for your actions? Why or why not?

THE PASSIONATE LEADER

If you don't have passion for the job in front of you, you'll never be an effective leader. The best leaders have a fire in their bones. They're so passionate about what they're doing that they're willing to work long hours to accomplish their goals.

They see their vision clearly and are 100% committed to making it a reality. Passion is infectious. When you, as a leader, are passionate about reaching your objectives, it causes others to be passionate as well.

Steve Jobs put it this way:

> YOU HAVE TO BE BURNING WITH AN IDEA, OR A PROBLEM, OR A WRONG THAT YOU WANT TO RIGHT. IF YOU'RE NOT PASSIONATE ENOUGH FROM THE START, YOU'LL NEVER STICK IT OUT.

Of course, this raises an important question: **what should you do if you're not passionate?**

If you're not passionate about the job before you, it means one of two things:

- **First, it could mean that you're doing the wrong job.** It's hard to be passionate about a job that you really don't care about. If you have zero passion for your job, it's a signal that you're probably in the wrong position and may be better served elsewhere.

- **Second, it could mean that you haven't set ambitious enough goals for yourself.** It's difficult to be passionate about small, mediocre goals. It's hard to care about goals that don't really add much to your personal or professional life.
    - On the other hand, big, audacious goals are much more motivating. They allow you to wake up every morning with a sense of purpose and drive. They push you to seek to achieve great things. If you're not feeling passionate, maybe you need to set bigger goals for yourself.

Ultimately, passion flows out of vision. If you have a clear vision of what you want to accomplish and can see the great good that it will accomplish, you'll be passionate. If, on the other hand, your vision is blurry and you're not sure what you want to accomplish, you won't be passionate at all.

THE PASSIONATE LEADER

Why is it so crucial that leaders be passionate?

What does it look like when a leader is passionate?

What are some of the causes of a lack of passion?

What does it mean that passion flows out of vision?

There are few things that a leader needs more than courage. The decisions you make as a leader will result in you being evaluated by others. They will criticize you from time to time. Sometimes you'll take action and it simply won't pan out.

Maya Angelou said, *"Courage is the most important of all the virtues because without courage, you can't practice any other virtue consistently."*

This is critical to understand. **If you're not courageous as a leader, you simply won't do any of the other things necessary to be a good leader.**

- You won't take appropriate risks because you're afraid of missing the mark.
- You won't suggest new ideas because you're afraid they'll be shot down.
- You won't take bold action because you might be judged by others.

There will be times when you simply don't know what the outcome of a particular action will be. In those moments, you'll be tempted to avoid acting at all.

It's those moments when courage is needed more than ever. You need the courage to act boldly, regardless of the outcome.

William Faulkner said it this way, "You cannot swim for new horizons until you have courage to lose sight of the shore."

As an effective leader, there will be times when you lose sight of the shore. When you're launching a totally new initiative. When you're introducing a new product that's unlike anything you've ever done before. When you're trying to create a new team to tackle a new, difficult project.

If you're going to achieve great things as a leader, you must have the courage to lose sight of the shore. To keep going even when you're not sure exactly how things are going to work out.
If you display great courage in the face of adversity, people will follow you. They'll admire and be inspired by your courage and want to emulate you.

THE COURAGEOUS LEADER

What is courage?

Why must a leader be courageous?

What happens when a leader is not courageous?

How can you grow in courage as a leader?

Integrity means always being consistent with your values. It means saying what you'll do and doing what you'll say. It means you have strong moral values and that you hold fast to those moral values in every situation.

If you don't have integrity, your followers will quickly abandon you. They'll see that what you say is different from what you do. That you don't have any particular morals guiding your actions. That the ends always justify the means.

Steven Covey said, "Moral authority comes from following universal and timeless principles like honesty, integrity, treating people with respect."

Do you want to have a sense of authority with those on your team? Do you want them to respect you? Do you want them to do what you ask without grumbling and arguing? Then be a person of integrity.

There will be times when you're faced with ethical dilemmas. In those moments, you have two options:

- Act with integrity and gain the respect of those under you.
- Act without integrity and lose the trust of your followers.

Without integrity, those under you simply won't trust you. They won't have confidence that you'll do what you say. They won't be confident that you have their best interests in mind.

Rather, they'll worry that you're asking them to do something for selfish, personal reasons rather than their own good and the good of the company.

THE LEADER WITH INTEGRITY

What is integrity?

How do you know if a person has integrity?

Why is integrity so important for a leader?

What are the consequences if a leader does not have integrity?

THE EMOTIONALLY INTELLIGENT LEADER

itelligent

Emotional intelligence is the ability to understand and manage both your own emotions and the emotions of those around you. It's the ability to understand why you're feeling a certain way in a particular situation and to understand why others might be feeling a particular way.

There will be many times when you find yourself in difficult, stressful, emotionally laden situations.

In those moments, **it's essential that you be able to understand why you're feeling a particular way and then respond appropriately.** If you simply fly off the handle and explode emotionally, you'll lose the respect and trust of those under you. You must be able to manage your emotions appropriately and handle emotionally difficult situations.

In the same way, you must also be able to understand why others are feeling specific emotions. This skill, often called Emotional IQ, allows you to see things through the eyes of others. It enables you to put yourself in someone else's shoes and experience the same emotions they are.

If you're unable to understand the emotions of others, you won't be able to effectively navigate highly emotional situations. You'll make decisions without considering the feelings of others, which can cause significant damage to your relationships.

The best leaders are able to keep a close handle on their own emotions and to help others manage their own volatile emotions.

THE EMOTIONALLY INTELLIGENT LEADER

What is emotional intelligence?

What are the benefits of having emotional intelligence?

What happens when a leader doesn't have emotional intelligence?

THE HUMBLE LEADER

Many people think that leaders must be proud, brash, and always right. In fact, the opposite is true. The best leaders are humble, listen, and are willing to admit when they're wrong.

Humility is one of the keys to great leadership.
A proud leader is in danger of blind spots. They are convinced that they are always right. They're sure that their way is the best way. They feel like they don't need to listen to the opinions of others.

This is a recipe for disaster.

A humble leader, on the other hand, is set up for success.

WHAT DOES HUMBLE LEADERSHIP LOOK LIKE?

Listening. The humble leader listens to the opinions and feedback of others. They don't assume that their ideas are always the best.

Asking for feedback. A humble leader asks those around him for constructive feedback. They realize that they don't know everything and need the valuable advice of others.

Admitting wrongs. Every leader makes mistakes. The best, most humble leaders admit when they've made mistakes. This creates an environment where others feel like they too can admit their mistakes.

Respect. The truly humble leader is respectful of others. They value the insights and opinions of others and do everything they can to respect what others bring to the table.

St. Augustine said, *"Do you wish to rise? Begin by descending. You plan a tower that will pierce the clouds? Lay first the foundation of humility."*

Humility is fundamental to success as a leader. Leaders who are humble thrive, while leaders who are proud ultimately falter.

THE HUMBLE LEADER

Why is humility so essential for effective leadership?

What are some indicators that a leader is humble?

What does proud leadership look like?

Why are proud leaders setting themselves up for failure?

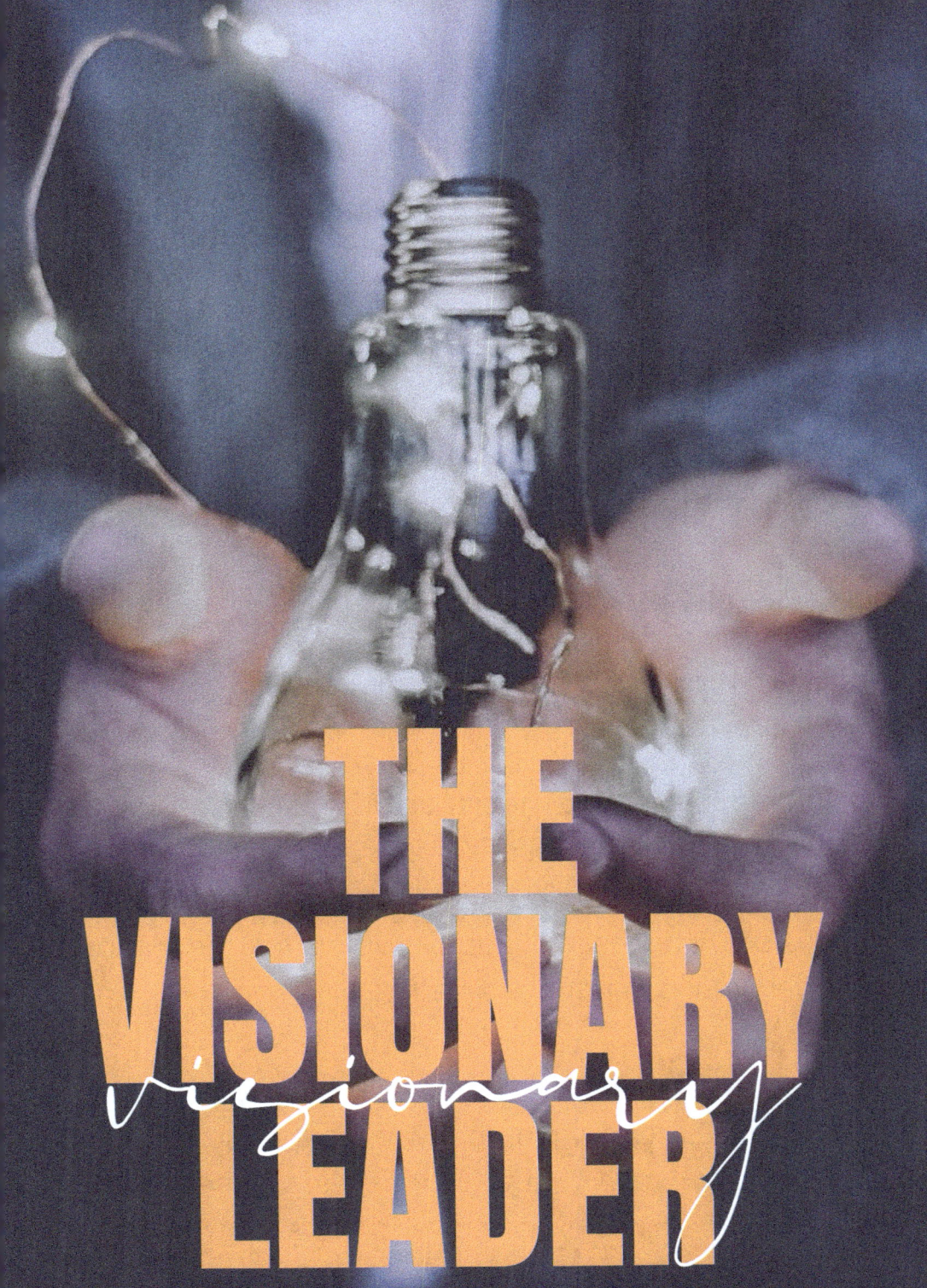

A leader is someone who moves people to take action. A leader helps others get from point A to point B. A leader looks forward into the future, sees good outcomes, and then helps people move toward those good outcomes.

In other words, a leader has vision. A leader doesn't merely organize people, resources, and efforts, although that's certainly necessary. A leader is able to peer into the future, see how certain actions will produce specific outcomes, and then motivate others to take those actions.

A POWERFUL VISION HAS FOUR SPECIFIC ELEMENTS:

It captures the heart and imagination. First and foremost, a leader's vision is able to capture the hearts and imaginations of their followers. Those who hear a positive vision for the future very much want to be a part of it.

It must be vivid. A leader must be able to paint a vivid picture of where they want to go. They should be able to communicate the benefits of their vision in clear, concrete, and powerful ways.

It must be achievable. While it's essential that the vision stretch others, it also must be achievable. If it's clearly not achievable, then they won't want to be a part of it.

It must be future-oriented. The leader looks into the future and sees what's possible. They can see a future that's better than the present and they can move others toward that future.

It's important to note that you won't be able to get people on board with your vision if you don't possess the qualities already mentioned. If you're not confident in your vision, others won't believe it's possible. If you're not passionate about your vision, they won't be excited to be part of it.

If you're not emotionally intelligent, you won't be able to effectively tap into people's emotions.

Whenever possible, communicate your vision to those around you. Theodore Hesburgh, the President of the University of Notre Dame, said:

"The very essence of leadership is that you have to have a vision. It's got to be a vision you articulate clearly and forcefully on every occasion."

If you want to get people on board with your vision, it's important to communicate clearly and forcefully as much as possible. Paint a picture of the good life that others will experience if your vision becomes reality.

James Kouzes and Barry Posner put it this

> "THERE'S NOTHING MORE DEMORALIZING THAN A LEADER WHO CAN'T CLEARLY ARTICULATE WHY WE'RE DOING WHAT WE'RE DOING."

Clearly, you don't want those following you to be demoralized. How do you prevent this? By clearly articulating the why behind the actions you're asking people to take.

THE VISIONARY LEADER

What does it mean that the best leaders have vision?

What happens when a leader doesn't have vision?

What are the elements of an effective vision?

How do you get others on board with your vision?

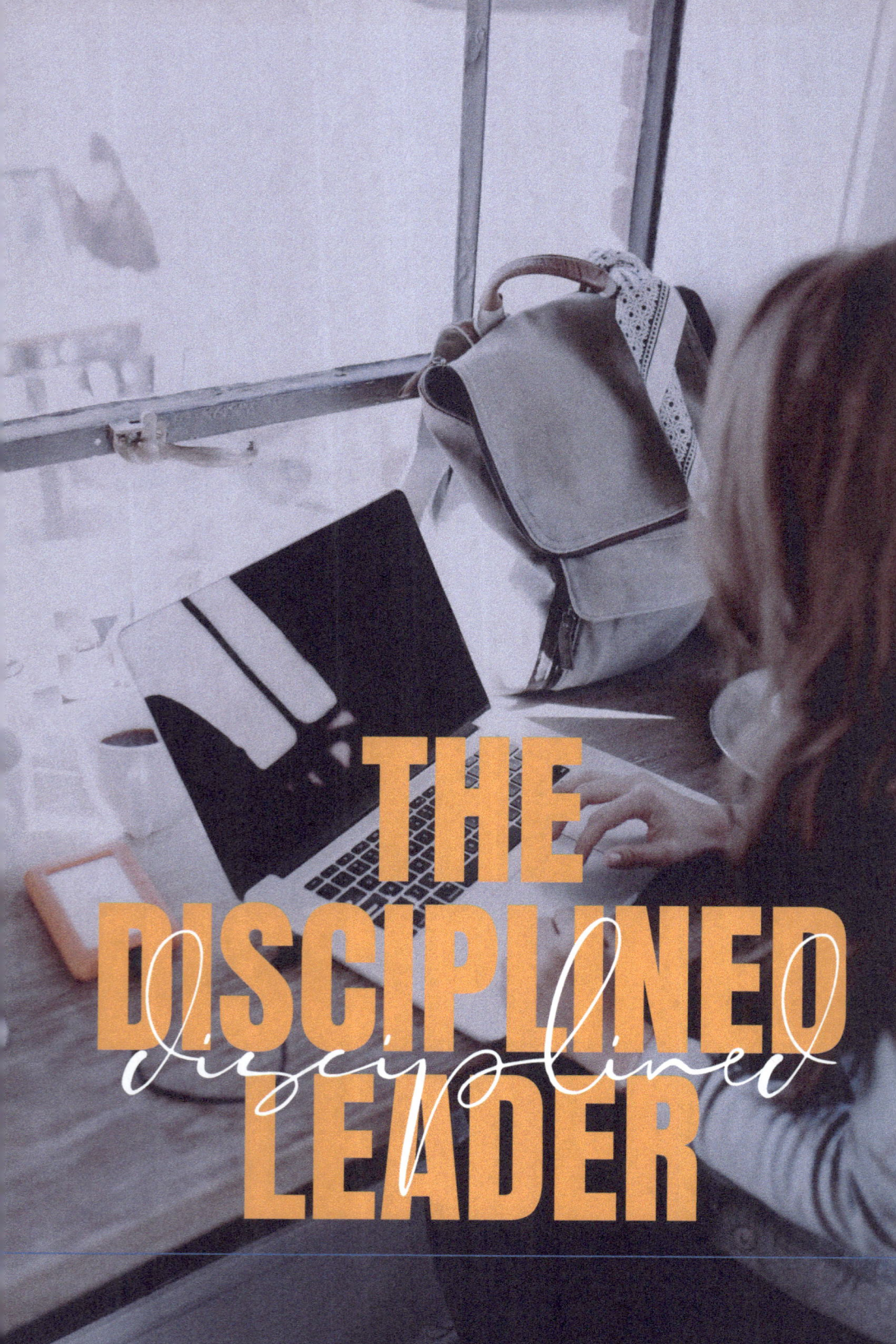

When it comes to leadership, discipline does not mean punishing people. Rather, discipline refers to being in complete control of oneself. A highly effective leader must be self-disciplined in all areas.

Discipline should encompass every area of the leader's life.

CONSIDER THESE AREAS:

1. **Health.** A leader knows that they must be in good health if they're going to effectively lead others. They discipline themselves to eat in healthy ways, exercise, and make other smart health-related choices.

   - **ASK YOURSELF THESE QUESTIONS: DO YOU...**
     - EAT HEALTHY FOODS?
     - REGULARLY EXERCISE?
     - GET SUFFICIENT SLEEP?

2. **Time.** Perhaps more than anything else, a leader must be disciplined with their time. They must be able to get things done efficiently, focusing on the job in front of them and making swift progress through their to-do list. It's easy to get sidetracked during the day, but the best leaders are able to maintain focus.

- **ASK YOURSELF THESE QUESTIONS: DO YOU...**
  - ALLOW YOURSELF TO BE EASILY DISTRACTED DURING THE DAY?
  - HAVE SPECIFIC GOALS YOU'RE FOCUSED ON ACHIEVING?
  - HAVE A SYSTEM FOR ENSURING THAT YOU MAKE PROGRESS ON YOUR TO-DO LIST?

3. **Vision.** The leader is disciplined to stay focused on their vision. They don't let other "shiny" objects distract them from their ultimate purpose and vision. They ensure that they and those who follow them stay laser-focused on getting the right things done all the time.

- **ASK YOURSELF THESE QUESTIONS: DO YOU...**
  - HAVE A SINGLE-MINDED FOCUS ON YOUR OVERALL VISION?
  - BECOME EASILY DISTRACTED FROM YOUR MOST IMPORTANT TASKS?
  - CONSISTENTLY REMIND BOTH YOURSELF AND YOUR FOLLOWERS OF YOUR VISION?

Jim Rohn said, *"Discipline is the bridge between goals and accomplishment."*

In other words, you'll never achieve your highest and greatest goals if you're not disciplined. If, on the other hand, you're able to hold yourself to the highest standards, you'll achieve success beyond your wildest dreams.

THE DISCIPLINED LEADER

What are the characteristics of a disciplined leader?

Why is discipline so important for a leader?

What are some areas in which a leader must have discipline?

What are the consequences if a leader doesn't have discipline?

The greatest leaders, the ones who achieve the most, the ones who inspire the most people, are those who communicate clearly, powerfully, and effectively. Consider great leaders throughout history: Winston Churchill, John F. Kennedy, Nelson Mandela. What do they all have in common? The ability to communicate their vision with passion, zeal, clarity, and force. They all were able to inspire people to become bigger and better versions of themselves.

THE GREATEST LEADERS, THE ONES WHO ACHIEVE THE MOST, THE ONES WHO INSPIRE THE MOST PEOPLE, ARE THOSE WHO COMMUNICATE CLEARLY, POWERFULLY, AND EFFECTIVELY.

Consider the classic speech, The Gettysburg Address, by Abraham Lincoln. It is only 272 words long and it only took him a few minutes to deliver it. And yet, because he took a significant amount of time to shape and clarify it, it was one of the most powerful speeches ever given. Even to this day, it is still highly emotional and motivating.

HOW CAN YOU ENSURE THAT YOUR COMMUNICATIONS ARE BOTH CLEAR AND POWERFUL? CONSIDER USING THE 7 "CS" OF COMMUNICATION:

Clear. Every aspect of your communications must be clear, both to you and to your audience.

Complete. Your communications should include as much relevant information as possible, so the listener can get a complete picture.

Concise. Your sentences, paragraphs, and main points should all be appropriately concise.

Concrete. Use concrete language rather than abstract.

Courteous. Your communications should be courteous to your audience, considering both their feelings and viewpoints.

Correct. Each statement in your communications should be correct.

Considerate. Your communications are considerate of how the audience thinks and thus presents information in ways that are relevant and helpful.

The greatest leaders take the necessary time to craft their communications so that they are as powerful and impactful as possible. They don't rush things because they realize that few things are more powerful than their words.

The Center For Creative Leadership puts it this way:

"Communication is a core leadership function. Effective communication and effective leadership are closely intertwined. Leaders need to be skilled communicators in countless relationships at the organizational level, in communities and groups, and sometimes on a global scale.
You need to think with clarity, express ideas, and share information with a multitude of audiences."

If you want to be a great leader, work hard to strengthen your communication skills. Without the ability to communicate clearly, you simply can't move people from point A to point B. You won't be able to paint a vivid picture of your vision or inspire others to take great action.

THE COMMUNICATING LEADER

Why is effective communication so crucial for leadership?

What are the characteristics of effective communication?

What happens when a leader can't communicate effectively?

Which of your communication skills would you like to strengthen?

KNOW, GO, AND SHOW THE WAY

John C. Maxwell said, *"A leader is one who knows the way, goes the way, and shows the way."*

THIS IS THE ESSENCE OF LEADERSHIP.

A leader has vision and can see the way to go.

A leader is self-motivated, self-disciplined, passionate, and courageous enough to do the hard work necessary to make their vision a reality.

A leader constantly communicates their vision to others, showing them the way to go.

We covered a lot of ground in this book. The 11 characteristics of an effective leader are:

SELF-MOTIVATION
CONFIDENCE
ACCOUNTABILITY
PASSION
COURAGE
INTEGRITY
EMOTIONAL INTELLIGENCE
HUMILITY
VISION
DISCIPLINE
COMMUNICATION

The good news is that you can grow in all of these areas. You can become an effective leader. The more you focus on growing in these areas, the better you'll become as a leader and the more people will want to follow you. As more people follow you, you'll have more opportunities to grow as a leader.

It's a powerful cycle that can cause you to grow leaps and bounds.

So, don't wait any longer. Start leading today. Others are waiting to follow you.

NOTES

8
DAILY HABITS OF
OUTSTANDING
leaders

The next few pages will guide you through 8 daily habits and how you can integrate them into your day.

Let's get moving....

MORNING ROUTINE

How do you usually feel when you wake up in the morning? Would you like to feel differently? What can you do to inspire the feelings you desire?

What is one practice you'd like to add to your morning or daily routine?

ACT ACCORDING TO YOUR VALUES

In the first column, write down your top five core values (it's okay if they change over time). In the second column, write down one or two actions that you associate with the core value you have selected.

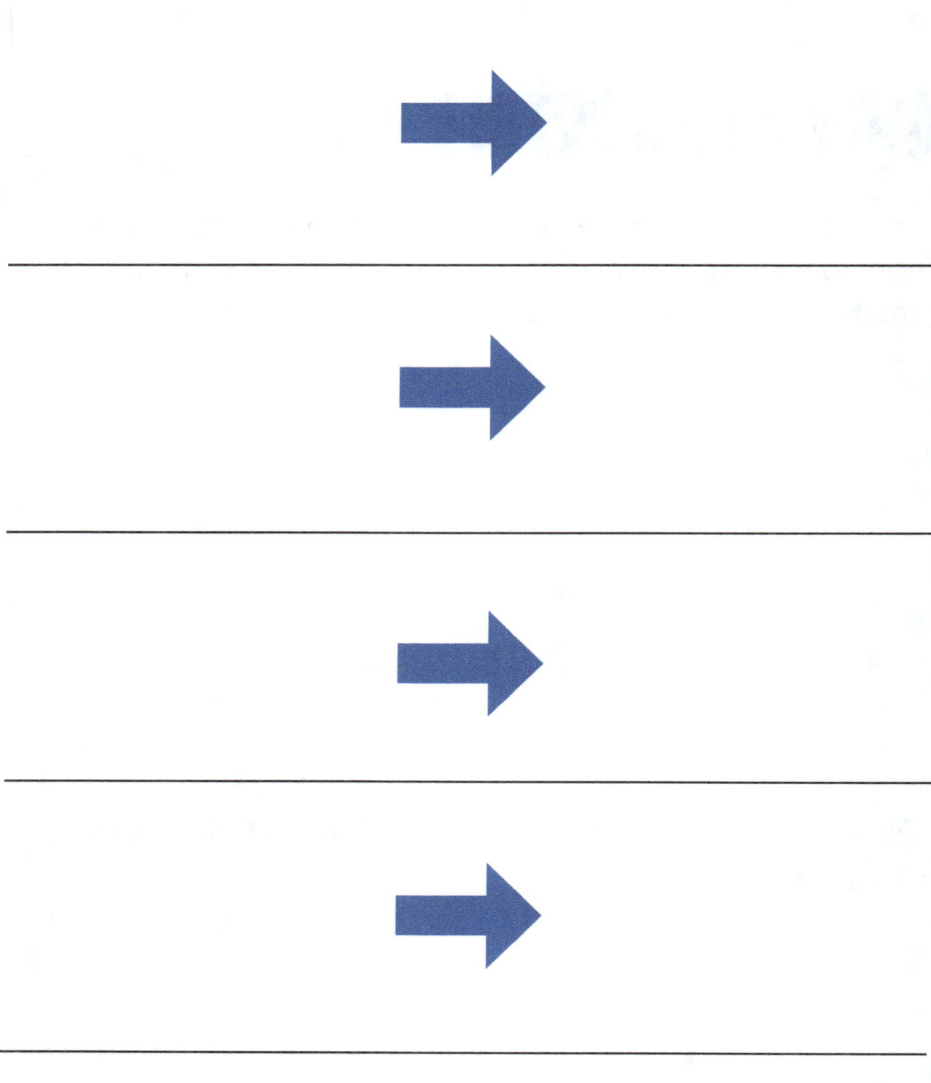

PROFESSIONAL DEVELOPMENT

What is one activity you'd like to add to your day that would encourage more learning? Are you growing daily? Are you ready for massive success?

PRACTICE MINDFULNESS

Do you currently have opinions about meditation? What is your experience with meditation? Is there anything that makes you nervous about meditation?
What is a mindfulness activity you might like?

WRITE AFFIRMATIONS

Do you take time daily to write in a journal? What are you grateful for? What is your vision? What does your life look like 5 years from now?

HELP OTHERS

What is one obstacle you may face when giving others direction? How might you move past that obstacle? Are you doing enough? Are you helping enoughother people?

BE AUTHENTIC

What is one way you've been inauthentic in a professional setting? How can you move toward authenticity in your leadership style?

SELF REFLECTION

What do you need to let go of in order for your greater calling to come forth? How can you release the small you, in order for your greater you to show up? How can you listen deeper to your greatest self?

MORE ABOUT Nakia

NAKIA EVANS

CORE STRENGTHS

Nakia's strongest skills are listening, building teams, leading groups and collaborating with leaders. Nakia is passionate about community outreach and education. Since 2002, Nakia has held a career as a real estate agent and coach. As a Visionary Leader & Self Improvement Coach in the Greater Baltimore area, Nakia emphasizes education, collaboration and wealth building.

In 2020, Nakia gave her corporate job back, reBranded, and started to build her family's legacy with other leaders in and outside of the real estate industry.

Nakia is committed to providing exceptional service to all, including her real estate team at eXp Realty.

CONNECT WITH NAKIA!

Instagram & Twitter:
@movingwithnakia
Facebook & Linked In:
@Nakia Evans
www.NakiaEvans.com

Nakia takes a nurturing and ethical approach to everything that comes her way. Nakia is known for being prepared, professional and productive.

Many clients and agents look to Nakia for guidance regarding innovative marketing strategies, honing their negotiation skills, assistance in making clear & concise decisions, and gathering & communicating reliable answers throughout the home buying & selling process. During each relationship, she guides and teaches along the way.

Nakia has always been an active member of the community she lives and serves in.

She is a REALTOR®, mentor, wife, friend, and trusted leader to all who know her, personally & professionally.

Most importantly, Nakia is a proud daughter, mother, grandmother, sister, aunt and cousin!

Favorite Motto:
- Let's Get Moving!

Favorite saying:
- Let's Be Clear!

Daily Affirmation:
- I am more than enough!

Please visit NakiaEvans.com to connect, find more resources & to build a new relationship with Nakia!

www.ingramcontent.com/pod-product-compliance
Lightning Source LLC
Chambersburg PA
CBHW070808220526
45466CB00002B/595